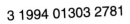

# Rolling

by **Dana Meachen Rau**

Reading Consultant: Nanci R. Vargus, Ed. D.

**Marshall Cavendish**
Benchmark
New York

# Picture Words

bike

bowling ball

flowers

goal

grass

handlebars

 pins

 scooter

 skateboard

 skates

soccer ball

wagon

wheels

Things that are round roll.

Things with roll.

A  can roll.

A boy kicks it to the .

A  can roll.

It pushes down the 🎳.

 can roll.

Kids skate on a path.

A  can roll.

A boy rides on the top.

A  can roll.

A girl holds the  .

A  can roll.

It rolls down the hill.

A  can roll.

It holds  for the garden.

You can roll, too.

You can roll in the  .

# Words to Know

**garden**  a place where plants grow

**kick**     (kik)
           to move with your feet

**round**   smooth with no corners

# Find Out More

## Books

Douglas, Lloyd G. *What Is a Wheel and Axle?* (Welcome Books). Danbury, CT: Children's Press, 2002.

Gibbons, Gail. *My Soccer Book*. New York: HarperCollins, 2001.

Johns, Linda. *I Can Bowl!* (Rookie Reader). Danbury, CT: Children's Press, 2003.

Schlepp, Tammy J. *Things on Wheels*. Brookfield, CT: Copper Beach Books, 2000.

## Videos

Harkes, John. *Let's Play Soccer*. ESPN Home Video.

## Web Sites

**Games Kids Play**
http://www.gameskidsplay.net/

**The History of the Wheel: The Wild History of Roller Skates**
http://inventors.about.com/library/weekly/aa050997.htm

**Kids Health: Bike Safety**
http://kidshealth.org/kid/watch/out/bike_safety.html

## About the Author

Dana Meachen Rau is an author, editor, and illustrator. A graduate of Trinity College in Hartford, Connecticut, she has written more than one hundred books for children, including nonfiction, biographies, early readers, and historical fiction. She likes to roll down the grassy hill in her backyard in Burlington, Connecticut.

## About the Reading Consultant

Nanci R. Vargus, Ed.D, wants all children to enjoy reading. She used to teach first grade. Now she works at the University of Indianapolis. Nanci helps young people become teachers. She likes to push her granddaughter in her stroller.

Marshall Cavendish Benchmark
99 White Plains Road
Tarrytown, NY 10591-9001
www.marshallcavendish.us

All Internet sites were correct at the time of printing.

Library of Congress Cataloging-in-Publication Data

Rau, Dan Meachen, 1971–
Rolling / by Dana Meachen Rau.
     p. cm. — (Benchmark rebus)
Summary: "Easy to read text with rebuses explores things that roll"—Provided by publisher.
Includes bibliographical references.
ISBN-13: 978-0-7614-2314-0
ISBN-10: 0-7614-2314-1
Vocabulary—Juvenile literature. I. Title. II. Series.
PE1449.R3394 2006
428.1—dc22
     2005032454

Editor: Christine Florie
Editorial Director: Michelle Bisson
Art Director: Anahid Hamparian
Series Designer: Virginia Pope

Photo research by Connie Gardner

Rebus images, with the exception of handlebars, provided courtesy of *Dorling Kindersley*.

Cover photo by Yellow Dog Productions/Image Bank/*Getty Images*

The photographs in this book are used with permission and through the courtesy of:
*PhotoEdit*: p. 5 Michael Newman; p. 13 Tony Freeman; p. 21 Michael Newman; *Corbis*: p. 7 Tim Klusaiaas; p. 15, p. 17, p. 19 Royalty-Free; *Peter Arnold, Inc.*: p. 9 Jodi Jacobson; *SuperStock*: p. 11 Greer and Associates, Inc.

Printed in Malaysia
1  3  5  6  4  2